THERE'S TREASURE EVERYWHERE

THERE'S TREASURE EVERYWHERE

A Calvin and Hobbes Collection by Bill Watterson

Scholastic Inc.

New York Toronto London Auckland Sydney

ISBN 0-590-97208-1

12 11 10 9 8 7 6 5 4 3 2 1   6 7 8 9/9 0 1/0

Printed in the U.S.A.   08

First Scholastic printing, September 1996

THAT CLOUD DOES IMPRESSIONS!

CALVIN, WOULD YOU SET THE TABLE FOR ME PLEASE?

MM... I DON'T THINK SO. I'M NOT ENTHUSIASTIC ABOUT SETTING THE TABLE.

I DON'T THINK YOU SHOULD HAVE TO DO SOMETHING UNLESS YOU'RE ENTHUSIASTIC ABOUT IT.

calvin and HOBBES by WATTERSON
3
2
..SIGHHH...
THREE PLUS TWO....CALVIN?

AT THIS ROOM, TIME ENTERS A NO-PASSING ZONE.

LET GO OF ME, YA BIG GALOOT! WHY DON'T YOU PICK ON SOMEBODY YOUR OWN SIZE?!

They'd hit back.

..I GUESS THAT HAS A CERTAIN UNETHICAL LOGIC TO IT...

Calvin and Hobbes — by WATTERSON

Panel 1: TODAY AT SCHOOL, I TRIED TO DECIDE WHETHER TO CHEAT ON MY TEST OR NOT.

Panel 2: I WONDERED, IS IT BETTER TO DO THE RIGHT THING AND FAIL ...OR IS IT BETTER TO DO THE WRONG THING AND SUCCEED?

Panel 3: ON THE ONE HAND, UNDESERVED SUCCESS GIVES NO SATISFACTION. ...BUT ON THE OTHER HAND, WELL-DESERVED FAILURE GIVES NO SATISFACTION EITHER.

Panel 4: OF COURSE, MOST EVERYBODY CHEATS SOME TIME OR OTHER. PEOPLE ALWAYS BEND THE RULES IF THEY THINK THEY CAN GET AWAY WITH IT. ...THEN AGAIN, THAT DOESN'T JUSTIFY *MY* CHEATING.

THEN I THOUGHT, LOOK, CHEATING ON ONE LITTLE TEST ISN'T SUCH A BIG DEAL. IT DOESN'T HURT ANYONE.

...BUT THEN I WONDERED IF I WAS JUST RATIONALIZING MY UNWILLINGNESS TO ACCEPT THE CONSEQUENCE OF NOT STUDYING.

STILL, IN THE REAL WORLD, PEOPLE CARE ABOUT SUCCESS, NOT PRINCIPLES. ...THEN AGAIN, MAYBE THAT'S WHY THE WORLD IS IN SUCH A MESS. WHAT A DILEMMA!

SO WHAT DID YOU DECIDE?

NOTHING. I RAN OUT OF TIME AND I HAD TO TURN IN A BLANK PAPER.

ANYMORE, SIMPLY ACKNOWLEDGING THE ISSUE IS A MORAL VICTORY.

WELL, IT JUST SEEMED WRONG TO CHEAT ON AN ETHICS TEST.

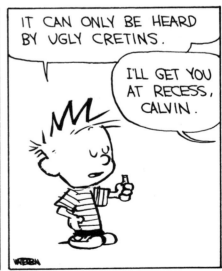

 WHAT IF SOMEBODY CALLS US "A PAIR O' PATHETIC PERIPATETICS"?!

 I'VE NEVER HEARD OF ANYONE TAKING THE TROUBLE TO RHYME WEIRD INSULTS.

BUT SHOULDN'T WE HAVE A READY RETORT?

 I'M DOING A CROSSWORD PUZZLE. NUMBER THREE ACROSS SAYS "BIRD."

HMM..

 I'VE GOT IT! "YELLOW-BELLIED SAPSUCKER"!

BUT THERE ARE ONLY FIVE BOXES.

 I KNOW. THESE IDIOTS MAKE YOU WRITE REAL SMALL.

YOUR NEW POLLS ARE IN, DAD.

MM.

A VAST MAJORITY OF HOUSEHOLD SIX-YEAR-OLDS SAY YOU'RE NOT LIVING UP TO THEIR EXPECTATIONS OF FATHERHOOD.

WHAT WERE THEIR EXPECTATIONS?

THAT YOU'D BE MORE LIKE AN AUTOMATIC TELLER MACHINE.

WHERE DO YOU POLLSTERS FIND THESE RESPONDENTS?

THE MORE YOU KNOW, THE HARDER IT IS TO TAKE DECISIVE ACTION.

ONCE YOU BECOME INFORMED, YOU START SEEING COMPLEXITIES AND SHADES OF GRAY.

YOU REALIZE THAT NOTHING IS AS CLEAR AND SIMPLE AS IT FIRST APPEARS. ULTIMATELY, KNOWLEDGE IS PARALYZING.

BEING A MAN OF ACTION, I CAN'T AFFORD TO TAKE THAT RISK.

YOU'RE IGNORANT, BUT AT LEAST YOU ACT ON IT.

HAVE YOU BEEN READING ABOUT THE "ELECTRONIC SUPERHIGHWAY"?

PRETTY SOON, COMPUTERS, TELEPHONES AND TVs WILL ALL BE HOOKED TOGETHER TO BRING INSTANTANEOUS, INTERACTIVE COMMUNICATION RIGHT INTO OUR HOMES!

BUT DAD SAYS HE LIKED IT BETTER WHEN YOU HAD TO COMMUNICATE BY MAIL, AND YOU KNEW YOU WOULDN'T HEAR BACK FROM ANYBODY FOR AT LEAST A WEEK.

OF COURSE, YOUR DAD THINKS TRANSPORTATION SHOULD'VE STOPPED WITH THE BICYCLE.

I'M A 21ST-CENTURY KID TRAPPED IN A 19TH-CENTURY FAMILY.

WAIT! DON'T HIT ME! THERE'S SOMETHING ON YOUR BACK!

I'm sure.

I'M SERIOUS! IT'S A NOTE! YOUR MOM MUST'VE PINNED IT ON YOUR SHIRT.

What's it say?

IT SAYS, "SOMEBODY RUN THIS BOY OVER WITH A TRUCK."

IF I'M GOING TO GET CLOBBERED, I LIKE TO DESERVE IT.

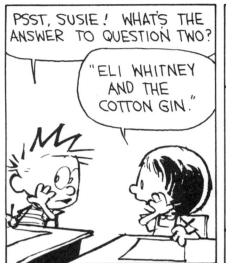

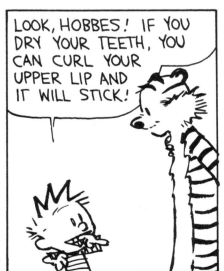

calvin and HObbEs by WATTERSON

I LOVE MY SCHOOL BOOKS. JUST THINK! PRETTY SOON WE'LL HAVE READ **ALL** OF THIS!

I LIKE TO READ AHEAD AND SEE WHAT WE'RE GOING TO LEARN NEXT. IT'S SO EXCITING TO KNOW STUFF.

HAVING A BOOK IS LIKE HAVING A GOOD FRIEND WITH YOU.

IF YOU FLIP THE PAGES OF **MY** BOOK, AN ANIMATED T. REX DRIVES THE BATMOBILE AND EXPLODES!

SOMETIMES I THINK BOOKS ARE THE ONLY FRIENDS WORTH HAVING.

I DON'T NEED TO STUDY! I DON'T NEED TO LEARN!

I CAN ALWAYS GET BY ON MY GOOD LOOKS AND CHARM!

I DON'T HEAR YOU CONCURRING, HAIRBALL BREATH.

TELL ME, IS IT STATIC ELECTRICITY THAT MAKES YOUR HAIR DO THAT?

NOWADAYS, ADS DON'T JUST SELL A PRODUCT. THEY SELL AN ATTITUDE! LOOK AT THIS ONE!

HERE'S A COOL GUY SAYING NOBODY TELLS HIM WHAT TO DO. HE DOES WHATEVER HE WANTS AND HE BUYS THIS PRODUCT AS A REFLECTION OF THAT INDEPENDENCE.

SO BASICALLY, THIS MAVERICK IS URGING EVERYONE TO EXPRESS HIS INDIVIDUALITY THROUGH CONFORMITY IN BRAND-NAME SELECTION?

WELL, IT SOUNDED MORE DEFIANT THE WAY *HE* SAID IT.

MM.

HERE'S ANOTHER AD WITH ATTITUDE.

THIS GUY DIDN'T LIKE HIS JOB, SO HE QUIT, AND NOW HE CLIMBS ROCKS! SEE, HE'S HIS OWN MAN! HE GRABS LIFE BY THE THROAT AND LIVES ON HIS OWN TERMS!

IF HE QUIT HIS JOB, I WONDER HOW HE AFFORDS THOSE EXPENSIVE ATHLETIC SHOES HE'S ADVERTISING.

MAYBE HIS MOM BOUGHT THEM FOR HIM.

I HOPE SHE'LL PAY HIS MEDICAL BILLS WHEN HE FALLS OFF THAT ROCK.

Calvin and Hobbes by Watterson

32

HOLD IT, MOE! BEFORE YOU WALLOP ME, I'M AFRAID YOU'LL HAVE TO SIGN THIS FORM.

What's this?

IT'S A STATEMENT ACKNOWLEDGING RESPONSIBILITY FOR YOUR BEHAVIOR.

YOU AGREE THAT HITTING ME ENTITLES ME TO UNLIMITED COMPENSATION FOR MEDICAL TREATMENT AS WELL AS REASONABLE DAMAGES FOR PAIN AND SUFFERING. YOU AFFIRM THAT YOU'RE INSURED FOR THESE COSTS AND...

NOBODY TAKES RESPONSIBILITY FOR HIS ACTIONS ANYMORE.

HERE, DAD. I'D LIKE YOU TO SIGN THIS FORM AND HAVE IT NOTARIZED.

"I, THE UNDERSIGNED DAD, ATTEST THAT I HAVE NEVER PARENTED BEFORE, AND INSOFAR AS I HAVE NO EXPERIENCE IN THE JOB,...

...I AM LIABLE FOR MY MISTAKES AND I AGREE TO PAY FOR ANY COUNSELING, IN PERPETUITY, CALVIN MAY REQUIRE AS A RESULT OF MY PARENTAL INEPTITUDE."

I DON'T SEE HOW YOU'RE ALLOWED TO HAVE A KID WITHOUT SIGNING ONE OF THOSE.

MISS WORMWOOD, I'D LIKE YOU TO SIGN THIS CONTRACT.

IT'S AN AGREEMENT THAT YOU'LL COMPENSATE ME FOR ANY LOSS OF JOB INCOME I MAY SUFFER AS AN ADULT BECAUSE OF A POOR FIRST-GRADE EDUCATION.

IF YOU GET A POOR FIRST-GRADE EDUCATION, IT WILL BE FROM *YOUR* LACK OF EFFORT, NOT MINE. GET BACK TO YOUR DESK.

BY GOLLY, *SOMEBODY* OUGHT TO PAY ME IF I DON'T LEARN ANYTHING.

HI SUSIE! WOULD YOU SIGN THIS LEGAL DOCUMENT?

WHAT IS IT?

IN ESSENCE, IT ANNULS OUR KNOWLEDGE OF EACH OTHER'S EXISTENCE AND IT PROHIBITS ANY FUTURE SOCIAL INTERACTION.

SPECIFICALLY, IT STATES THAT I'LL NEVER ASK YOU OUT ON A DATE, AND IT IMPOSES SEVERE PENALTIES ON ANY PARTY THAT ATTEMPTS TO ENGAGE THE OTHER IN CONVERSA...

IT'S ALMOST INSULTING HOW FAST SHE SIGNED THAT.

Calvin: HERE, HOBBES. I'VE DRAWN UP A FRIENDSHIP CONTRACT FOR YOU TO SIGN.

Hobbes: A CONTRACT?

Calvin: RIGHT. IT CODIFIES THE TERMS OF OUR FRIENDSHIP. YOU CAN RENEGOTIATE IN 20 YEARS.

Hobbes: PEOPLE ARE FRIENDS BECAUSE THEY *WANT* TO BE, NOT BECAUSE THEY *HAVE* TO BE!

Calvin: THAT'S WHAT THIS FIXES.

Hobbes: IF YOUR FRIENDS ARE CONTRACTUAL, YOU DON'T HAVE ANY.

Calvin: DAD, WHY DO MY EYES SHUT WHEN I SNEEZE?

Dad: IF YOUR LIDS WEREN'T CLOSED, THE FORCE OF THE EXPLOSION WOULD BLOW YOUR EYEBALLS OUT AND STRETCH THE OPTIC NERVE, SO YOUR EYES WOULD FLOP AROUND AND YOU'D HAVE TO POINT THEM WITH YOUR HANDS TO SEE ANYTHING.

Calvin: GROSS.

Calvin: HOW COME YOU KNOW SO MUCH?

Dad: IT'S ALL IN THE BOOK YOU GET WHEN YOU BECOME A FATHER.

CALVIN, THE MIGHTY TYRANNOSAUR, STANDS OVER HIS KILL AND ROARS TRIUMPHANTLY!

CALViN and HObbES by WATTERSON

THE STRUGGLE TO BRING DOWN HIS PREY HAS GIVEN CALVIN A MONSTROUS APPETITE!

WITH MASSIVE JAWS TWISTING VIOLENTLY AT THE CARCASS, HE RIPS APART GIGANTIC CHUNKS AND SWALLOWS THEM WHOLE! WHAT A DISGUSTING SPECTACLE OF SAVAGE GLUTTONY!

THAT'S ENOUGH FOR TONIGHT, CALVIN. YOU'RE GOING TO GET SICK IF YOU EAT ALL THAT.

BUT MOM, I *EARNED* IT!

DOGGONE IT, HE'S GOT ALL THE COVERS AGAIN.

ZZ

ZZ... HMM? OH YES, I'M *VERY* FOND OF CALVIN. ...PASS THE GRAVY, PLEASE. ZZZ.

BRRR..

ZZ

WHY SHOULD I TAKE A BATH? I'M JUST GOING TO GET DIRTY AGAIN.

WHY SHOULD I BRUSH MY TEETH? I'M JUST GOING TO EAT AGAIN.

WHY SHOULD I COMB MY HAIR? IT'S JUST GOING TO GET MESSED UP AGAIN.

I'D RATHER BE EFFICIENT THAN HYGIENIC.

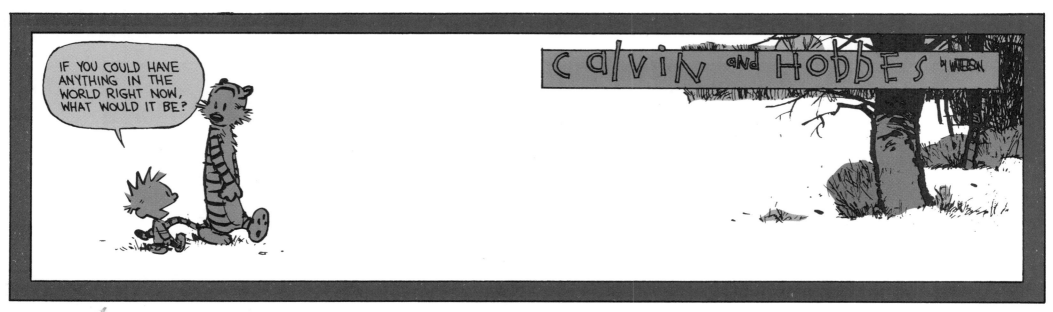

TALK ABOUT A FAILURE OF IMAGINATION! I'D ASK FOR A TRILLION BILLION DOLLARS, MY OWN SPACE SHUTTLE, AND A PRIVATE CONTINENT!

BBRRBBRBRBB
BEEP BEEP

BRRMMBB BRBBRB

GAAAAA!
OOMP

YOU MOVED UPWIND, SILLY! SHEESH, HUMAN SENSES AREN'T WORTH BEANS.

GET OFF ME, YOU PSYCHOTIC SAVAGE!

Calvin and Hobbes
by WATTERSON

YOUR NATURE PROGRAM IS ON. DON'T YOU WANT TO WATCH IT?

NO!

47

..AND SO, IN 1654...

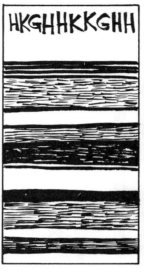

HKGHHKKGHH

MYSTERIOUS PLANET ZARTOK-3 APPEARS FROM...

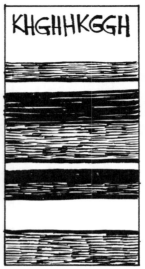

KHGHHKGGH

PAY ATTENTION!

WHEN YOU CHANGE THE CHANNEL, I DON'T THINK THE ORIGINAL PROGRAM SHOULD BE ABLE TO CHANGE IT BACK.

MOM, WHAT WAS I LIKE AS A BABY?

STINKY.

STINKY??

STINKY.

IT'S ALWAYS SHOCKING TO SEE ONE'S EXISTENCE REDUCED TO A BLURB.

caLviN aNd HobbEs by WATTERSON

BOY, IT'S COLD OUT! IT'S A PERFECT DAY FOR US SNOWMEN!

WHAT A GREAT SPOT FOR A FEW FEET OF SNOW!

YES SIR, A SNOWMAN LIKE ME COULD BE REAL HAPPY HERE!

.. SIGHHHH...

THE DECOY ISN'T WORKING?

MAYBE DUCKS ARE EASIER TO FOOL THAN SNOW.

THE THINKING CAP IS ALL SET! LET'S TURN IT ON!

CLICK.

BRZAP.

DID IT WORK?

I THINK SO.

I FEEL SMARTER ALREADY.

WHAT HAPPENED TO YOUR HEAD?!?

EVIDENTLY, AN UNANTICIPATED PHYSIOLOGICAL CONSEQUENCE OF CEREBRAL AUGMENTATION. MY BRAIN SWELLED.

IF YOUR HATS DON'T FIT, WILL YOU GIVE THEM TO ME?

MY POWERFUL BRAIN IS UNRAVELING THE MYSTERIES OF THE UNIVERSE.

IT'S AMAZING! ALL NATURAL LAWS CAN BE REDUCED TO ONE SIMPLE, UNIFYING EQUATION!

REALLY? WHAT IS IT?

ALREADY MY POWERFUL BRAIN IS BORED WITH SUCH SIMPLE PROBLEMS AND IS NOW WORKING ON WHY GIRLS ARE SO OBNOXIOUS.

NOW THAT THE THINKING CAP HAS ENLARGED YOUR BRAIN, YOU CAN WRITE YOUR HOMEWORK PAPER.

I CONCUR.

CALVIN, DINNERTIME.

UH OH. WAIT UNTIL YOUR PARENTS SEE YOUR HEAD!

I AM APPLYING MY POWERFUL BRAIN TO THE DILEMMA.

I KNOW! WE'LL WRAP MY HEAD IN THIS BEDSHEET! *THAT* WILL ALLAY ANY SUSPICION!

YOUR POWERFUL BRAIN MUST KNOW SOMETHING I DON'T.

CALVIN, COME DOWN FOR DINNER! I'M NOT CALLING YOU AGAIN!

HURRY UP WITH THE TURBAN!

THERE.

SORRY I'M LATE. I WAS UNAVOIDABLY DETAINED.

CALVIN, WE DON'T EAT AT THE TABLE LOOKING LIKE THAT. TAKE OFF THE SHEET.

UH... HEH HEH.. ..UM..

THANK YOU.

I DON'T KNOW WHY I WORRY. THEY NEVER NOTICE ANYTHING.

I BROUGHT YOU SOME FISH FROM DINNER. OBVIOUSLY I DON'T NEED TO EAT BRAIN FOOD NOW.

OH BOY.

OK, LET'S GET DOWN TO BUSINESS. I'LL APPLY MY POWERFUL BRAIN TO THE PROBLEM OF MY HOMEWORK.

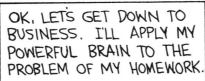

...HMMMMMM...

HOW'S IT GOING?

GOOD! I JUST REMEMBERED WHAT THE ASSIGNMENT WAS.

WATTERSON

MY POWERFUL BRAIN HAS COME UP WITH A TOPIC FOR MY PAPER.

GREAT.

I'LL WRITE ABOUT THE DEBATE OVER TYRANNOSAURS. WERE THEY FEARSOME PREDATORS OR DISGUSTING SCAVENGERS?

WHICH SIDE WILL YOU DEFEND?

OH, I BELIEVE THEY WERE FEARSOME PREDATORS, DEFINITELY.

HOW COME?

THEY'RE *SO* MUCH COOLER THAT WAY.

WATTERSON

LET'S SEE... TO ARGUE THAT TYRANNOSAURS WERE PREDATORS AND NOT SCAVENGERS, WE'LL NEED TO WRITE A BRIEF OVERVIEW OF CARNOSAUR EVOLUTION.

THEN WE'LL DELVE INTO SKELETAL STRUCTURE, SKULL DESIGN, ARM STRENGTH, POTENTIAL RUNNING SPEED, AND ENVIRONMENTAL FACTORS.

...BUT FIRST, WE'LL DRAW SOME PICTURES OF A T. REX EATING PEOPLE IN THE NATURAL HISTORY MUSEUM.

I NOTICE YOUR HEAD IS SHRINKING BACK TO NORMAL SIZE.

YOUR FOREHEAD IS BACK TO NORMAL.

THE BRAIN ENHANCEMENT MUST HAVE WORN OFF.

BUT YOU HAVEN'T WRITTEN YOUR PAPER YET.

OH, THAT'S THE EASY PART. THE *HARD* PART WAS GETTING A TOPIC AND MAKING THESE FUNNY DRAWINGS.

NOW ALL I HAVE TO DO IS WRITE EVERYTHING I KNOW ABOUT TYRANNOSAURS. IT'LL BE A BREEZE.

FOR ONCE I'M *GUARANTEED* A GOOD GRADE!

CALVIN, TIME FOR BED.

TIME FOR BED??

THAT'S WHAT I SAID.

BUT I HAVEN'T FINISHED MY PAPER FOR SCHOOL YET! I NEED MORE TIME!

HOW MUCH MORE DO YOU HAVE TO DO?

I JUST HAVE TO WRITE IT.

YOU MEAN IT'S BEDTIME AND YOU HAVEN'T EVEN STARTED WRITING YOUR PAPER FOR SCHOOL?! WHAT HAVE YOU BEEN *DOING* ALL EVENING??

WELL FIRST, HOBBES AND I INVENTED AND CONSTRUCTED A THINKING CAP THAT AUGMENTED MY BRAIN SO I COULD THINK UP A GOOD TOPIC, AND THEN WE DREW ILLUSTRATIONS OF ...

THAT DOESN'T SOUND LIKE A VERY GOOD TIME BUDGET TO ME.

I WASN'T EXPECTING TO GET AUDITED SO SOON.

MY PAPER IS ENTITLED, "TYRANNOSAURUS REX: FEARSOME PREDATOR OR LOATHSOME SCAVENGER?"

AHEM..." I SAY TYRANNOSAURS WERE PREDATORS, BECAUSE IT WOULD BE SO BOGUS IF THEY JUST ATE THINGS THAT WERE ALREADY DEAD. THE END."

I'M A CONCISE WRITER, OK?!?

MISS WORMWOOD WAS GOING TO GIVE ME A "D-" ON MY PAPER, BUT I TALKED TO HER AFTER CLASS AND TOLD HER HOW I RAN OUT OF TIME AND COULDN'T WRITE ALL I KNEW ABOUT TYRANNOSAURS.

SHE SAID I'D HAD PLENTY OF TIME TO DO THE ASSIGNMENT, BUT SHE ADMITTED THAT MAYBE I'D PICKED TOO COMPLEX A SUBJECT.

SO SHE RAISED MY GRADE TO A "D" AND TOLD ME I SHOULD TRY TO PICK REALISTIC GOALS AND PLAN MY TIME BETTER.

I GUESS WE LEARNED A LESSON, HUH?

I'LL SAY. SMOOTH-TALKING THE TEACHER REALLY PAYS OFF!

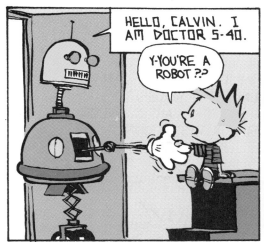

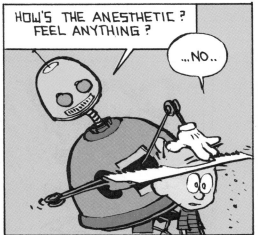

59

14...52...

POWAAUGH!!

YOU'RE SUPPOSED TO WAIT UNTIL I HIKE THE BALL!!

OOPS. SORRY.

DARN TIGERS. YOU CAN EXPLAIN THE RULES TO 'EM, BUT YOU CAN'T SUPPRESS THEIR SURPRISE POUNCE INSTINCT.

YESTERDAY DAD WENT OUT TO BUY A HARDCOVER NOVEL.

HE SAID HE WANTED TO READ SOMETHING LONG, RICH, AND THOUGHT-PROVOKING FOR A CHANGE, AND HE WANTED A CLOTH BINDING SO HIS BOOK COULD BE CARRIED AROUND AND REREAD LATER.

THEN HE SAID HE WAS GOING TO BUY THE BOOK WITH CASH, SO NOBODY COULD TRACE THE PURCHASE TO HIM AND EXPLOIT HIS INTERESTS FOR COMMERCIAL PURPOSES.

YOUR DAD'S GOING INTO THE FUTURE KICKING AND SCREAMING, ISN'T HE?

WHAT IF HE'S TURNING INTO SOME KIND OF SUBVERSIVE?

MOM, CAN I GET A BIG TATTOO? I WANT A WINGED SERPENT COILING AROUND ONE ARM, CLUTCHING A SHIP ON MY CHEST, WITH...

..UM... I MEAN... ...WELL...

..SIGHHHH..

DID YOU KNOW MOM CAN COMMUNICATE TELEPATHICALLY?

I'm gonna pound you at recess, Twinky.

YOU'D BETTER BE NICE TO ME, MOE.

Haw! Why?

BECAUSE SOMEDAY MY TAX DOLLARS WILL BE PAYING FOR YOUR PRISON CELL.

POW!

MY WHOLE PROBLEM IS MY LIPS MOVE WHEN I THINK.

YOU KNOW, EVERYTHING I AM... MY UNIQUE SPIRIT AND PERSONALITY... EVERYTHING THAT MAKES ME **ME** ...

...IS DEPENDENT ON THE PROPER FUNCTIONING OF THIS COMPLEX, FRAGILE AND MIRACULOUS CHUNK OF MEAT THAT IS MY BODY.

INTERESTING OBSERVATION.

WELL, IT JUST OCCURRED TO ME.

WAHOOOOOOO

THEY SAY THE WORLD IS A STAGE.

BUT OBVIOUSLY THE PLAY IS UNREHEARSED AND EVERYBODY IS AD-LIBBING HIS LINES.

MAYBE THAT'S WHY IT'S HARD TO TELL IF WE'RE IN A TRAGEDY OR A FARCE.

WE NEED MORE SPECIAL EFFECTS AND DANCE NUMBERS.

CalViN and HobbES
by WATTERSON

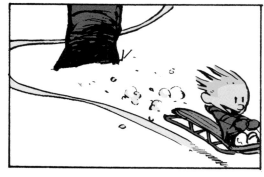

64

YEP, CHRISTMAS IS JUST AROUND THE CORNER.

AND WHAT BETTER WAY TO CELEBRATE A RELIGIOUS HOLIDAY THAN WITH A MONTH OF FRENZIED CONSUMERISM!

I'M SURPRISED OTHER RELIGIONS HAVEN'T PICKED UP ON THAT.

GETTING LOADS OF LOOT IS A VERY SPIRITUAL EXPERIENCE FOR ME.

DEAR SANTA,
EVERY YEAR AT THIS TIME I SEND YOU A LIST OF WHAT I WANT FOR CHRISTMAS.

AND EVERY YEAR YOU CALLOUSLY IGNORE IT AND BRING ME PRACTICAL THINGS I DON'T WANT AT ALL. WHAT'S THE DEAL?!

ARE YOU INSANE?? HAVE YOU GONE SENILE?? CAN'T YOU READ?? OR ARE YOU JUST A VINDICTIVE, TWISTED ELF BENT ON DESTROYING LITTLE KIDS' DREAMS?!?!

YOU MIGHT WANT TO SLEEP ON THIS ONE.

I KNOW, BUT IT FELT GOOD TO WRITE IT.

DEAR SANTA,
Last year I did not receive the 15,000 items I requested for Christmas.

I can only conclude that your secretarial staff must be a bunch of underpaid and woefully unprepared temps, and my letter was misfiled.

To avoid a similar disaster this year, just write me a check for five million dollars, and I'll buy the stuff myself.

SEE, **THIS** YEAR I WON'T BE DISAPPOINTED.

I'D LEAVE OUT THE PART ABOUT THE TEMPS.

DEAR SANTA,
HELLO, I AM CALVIN'S NEW BABY BROTHER, MELVILLE.

ENCLOSED is a list of what I want for Christmas. Please don't confuse MY list with Calvin's. There are TWO kids at this house now.

MAN, IF SANTA FALLS FOR THIS, I'LL ADD A NEW BROTHER EVERY YEAR!

"MELVILLE"?

Calvin and Hobbes
by Watterson

My hands were all shaky,
my face had gone pale.
A letter from Santa
just arrived in the mail!

It was hand-written
in old-fashioned ink pen.
It was handsomely printed
and dated twelve ten.

"Dear Calvin," it said,
"I'm writing because
this year I've repealed
my 'naughty/nice' laws.

So now, I urge you:
be vulgar and crude!
I *like* it when children
are boorish and rude!

Burp at the table!
Gargle your peas!
Never say 'thank you;
'you're welcome,' or
'please.'

Talk back to your mother!
Don't do as you're told!
Stick your tongue out
at your dad if he scolds!

Drive everyone crazy,
I really don't care!
Act like a jerk,
anytime, anywhere!

I'm changing the rules!
The *BAD* girls and boys
will be, from now on,
the ones who get toys!

Good little kids make
me sick, it's no joke.
Sincerely, signed Santa."

...And then I awoke.

I hate being good
(or trying to fake it).
Six days until Christmas!
I don't think I'll make it.

NO SNOW.

...WHICH MEANS I CAN'T PASTE ANYONE WITH A SNOWBALL... WHICH MEANS I'M GOOD... WHICH MEANS I'LL GET LOTS OF CHRISTMAS PRESENTS! HA!

NOTHING IN LIFE IS EVER EASY.

LOOK AT ALL THIS SNOW!

I'M BEING TESTED.

WE GOT THIS SNOW SO I'D BE TEMPTED TO SMACK SUSIE WITH A SLUSHBALL AND FORFEIT ALL MY CHRISTMAS PRESENTS.

TO EVALUATE MY CHARACTER, MY IMMEDIATE PLEASURE IS BEING PITTED AGAINST MY FUTURE GREED!

POOR SUSIE.

IT'S NOT A FOREGONE CONCLUSION!

THE DAY AFTER CHRISTMAS IS GOING TO BE EPIC.

THROWING THESE SNOWBALLS WOULD GIVE ME IMMEDIATE AND CERTAIN PLEASURE.

REFRAINING FROM THROWING THESE SNOWBALLS IN THE HOPE OF BEING REWARDED AT CHRISTMAS IS DELAYED AND **UN**CERTAIN PLEASURE.

AS USUAL, GOODNESS HARDLY PUTS UP A FIGHT.

 WHAT IF THERE IS NO SANTA CLAUS?

 YOU KNOW, A LOT OF THIS SANTA STUFF IS HARD TO BELIEVE. THE FLYING REINDEER, GOING AROUND THE WORLD IN ONE NIGHT, THE WHOLE CHIMNEY BIT...

 WHAT IF IT'S ALL SOME CRUEL HOAX AND I'M BEING GOOD FOR *NOTHING*?

 YOU'VE **ALWAYS** BEEN GOOD FOR NOTHING! IF HE EXISTS, SANTA WILL FORGIVE THIS ONE.

 I'M NOT BAD. I'M JUST...UM...

 ...EXUBERANT! THERE'S NOTHING WRONG WITH BEING EXUBERANT!

 HEADS UP! POW!

 GO ON, EXPLAIN THE SEMANTICS TO YOUR MOM. YIKES, SHE GOT HER WIND BACK AND SHE'S GAINING!

SANTA'S GONNA SKIP YOUR HOUSE FOR THAT, CALVIN!

I FIGURE THIS DOESN'T REALLY COUNT AGAINST ME, SINCE SHE'S SO SANCTIMONIOUS AND I KEEP MISSING.

HA HA! ACQUITTAL ON ALL CHARGES! COMPLETE EXONERATION! HA HA HA!

MERRY CHRISTMAS TO YOU TOO, DEAR.

PHEW, WHAT'S THAT SMELL? HAS SOMEONE BEEN EATING TUNA FISH AT THIS HORRIBLE HOUR?!

ARE YOU MAKING ANY RESOLUTIONS FOR THE NEW YEAR?

NOPE! I WANT EVERYTHING TO STAY THE SAME AS IT WAS **THIS** YEAR.

EVERYTHING?

RIGHT. THIS YEAR WAS LOUSY, BUT AT LEAST IT'S FAMILIAR.

I HATE CHANGE! IT'S TOO DISRUPTIVE! WHEN THINGS ARE DIFFERENT, YOU HAVE TO THINK ABOUT THE CHANGE AND DEAL WITH IT! I LIKE THINGS TO STAY THE SAME, SO I CAN TAKE EVERYTHING FOR GRANTED!

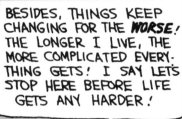

BESIDES, THINGS KEEP CHANGING FOR THE **WORSE**! THE LONGER I LIVE, THE MORE COMPLICATED EVERYTHING GETS! I SAY LET'S STOP HERE BEFORE LIFE GETS ANY HARDER!

FROM NOW ON, NO MORE CHANGE!

I'M BORED. LET'S DO SOMETHING DIFFERENT.

SOME THINGS DON'T CHANGE.

Y·YAWNN

THERE'S NO SEDATIVE LIKE SEEING A TIGER LYING IN THE SUN.

HEY DAD, WHY DON'T YOU CUT DOWN ALL THE TREES ON OUR HILL AND PUT IN A SKI LIFT?

BECAUSE A SKI LIFT WOULD BE UGLY, NOISY, AND COMPLETELY UNNECESSARY.

THE PROBLEM WITH DAD IS HE DOESN'T KNOW PROGRESS WHEN HE HEARS IT.

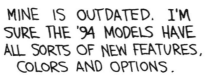

IF ANYONE HITS ME WITH A SNOWBALL, I'LL HIT **HIM** WITH 250 SNOWBALLS!

WHAT IF SOMEBODY HITS **YOU** WITH 250 SNOWBALLS?

..SIGHHH..

THIS WILL BE MY STRONGEST FORT EVER!

WITH THESE MASSIVE WALLS, I'LL BE SAFE FROM ANY ATTACK!

HELLLP!!

WE GOT SOME NEW SNOW LAST NIGHT! LET'S LOOK FOR ANIMAL TRACKS!

HERE ARE SOME BIRD TRACKS. LOOK, YOU CAN SEE WING IMPRESSIONS WHERE THEY TOOK OFF!

AND THESE ARE RABBIT TRACKS. LOOKS LIKE THEY WERE GOING PRETTY FAST.

NO WONDER! LOOK AT *THESE* TRACKS! SOMETHING WAS CHASING THEM ALL OVER THE PLACE!

Calvin and Hobbes by WATTERSON

HMM... BIG PADS... COULD BE A WOLF, BUT THERE ARE NO CLAW IMPRESSIONS. IT'S MORE LIKE A BOBCAT, OR A MOUNTAIN LION, OR...

..OR....

THIS EXPLAINS THE COLD WET FEET IN MY BED THIS MORNING.

THE SNOW WAS FALLING AND I THOUGHT, "THE BIRDS AND RABBITS AROUND HERE NEED SOME EXERCISE."

SOME PEOPLE COMPLAIN ALL THE TIME! THEY COMPLAIN ABOUT THE LEAST LITTLE THING!

IF SOMETHING BUGS THEM, THEY NEVER LET GO OF IT! THEY JUST GO ON AND ON, LONG AFTER ANYONE ELSE IS INTERESTED! IT'S JUST COMPLAIN, COMPLAIN, COMPLAIN! PEOPLE WHO GRIPE ALL THE TIME REALLY DRIVE ME NUTS!

YOU'D THINK THEY'D CHANGE THE SUBJECT AFTER A WHILE, BUT THEY NEVER DO! THEY JUST KEEP GRIPING UNTIL YOU START TO WONDER, "WHAT'S WRONG WITH THIS IDIOT?" BUT THEY GO ON COMPLAINING AND REPEATING WHAT THEY'VE ALREADY SAID!

MAYBE THEY'RE NOT VERY SELF-AWARE.

BOY, THAT'S *ANOTHER* THING THAT GETS ON MY NERVES!

WE NEED MORE EXTENSION CORDS.

CALVIN and HOBBES by WATTERSON

OK, THESE ARE MY FOOTPRINTS. HERE I STOP, HEAR SOMETHING, AND START TO TURN AROUND.

A FEW FEET FARTHER ON, HERE'S THE IMPRESSION OF MY BODY AS I HIT THE GROUND. THESE ARE THE POWDERED REMAINS OF THE SNOWBALL THAT HIT ME.

FROM THE ANGLE OF PARTICLE DISPERSEMENT, WE CAN TELL THE SNOWBALL WAS THROWN FROM OVER HERE, WHERE WE FIND...

...TIGER TRACKS.

THOSE COULD BE **ANYBODY'S** TIGER TRACKS.

POW!!

I MUST SAY, THE STINGING SNOW MAKES YOUR CHEEKS LOOK POSITIVELY RADIANT.

SOME PEOPLE SURE CAN'T TAKE A COMPLIMENT.

OUR LIVES ARE FILLED WITH MACHINES DESIGNED TO REDUCE WORK AND INCREASE LEISURE. WE HAVE MORE LEISURE THAN MAN HAS EVER HAD.

AND WHAT DO WE DO WITH THIS LEISURE? EDUCATE OURSELVES? TAKE UP NEW INTERESTS? EXPLORE? INVENT? CREATE?

DAD, I CAN'T HEAR THIS COMMERCIAL.

IF IT WERE UP TO DAD, LEISURE WOULD BE AS BAD AS WORK.

I *KNOW* I HAVE HAT HAIR, SO YOU DON'T NEED TO TELL ME.

ACTUALLY, IT'S NOT THAT DIFFERENT.

2. Where is Plymouth Rock?

I am not presently at liberty to divulge that information, as it might compromise our agents in the field.

I UNDERSTAND MY TESTS ARE POPULAR READING IN THE TEACHERS' LOUNGE.

Gimme a quarter, Twinky.

YOUR SIMIAN COUNTENANCE SUGGESTS A HERITAGE UNUSUALLY RICH IN SPECIES DIVERSITY.

What?

HERE YOU GO.

THAT WAS WORTH 25 CENTS.

LOOK, MOM, I MADE YOU SOME SUBTITLES.

HMM?

WHEN YOU'RE TALKING TO ME, YOU CHOOSE THE APPROPRIATE CARD TO TRANSLATE WHAT YOU'RE SAYING, AND PROP IT AGAINST YOUR FEET FOR ME TO READ.

FOR EXAMPLE, IF YOU SAY "GO TO BED *NOW*," YOU CAN USE THIS CARD, WHICH SAYS, "YOU'VE GOT TEN MINUTES UNTIL I BLOW MY STACK." SEE? THEN I'LL KNOW WHAT YOU MEAN.

YOU'VE GOT TEN MINUTES UNTIL I BLOW MY STACK.

I DON'T NEED TRANSLATION!

I'VE EVEN GOT SUBTITLES FOR PARENTISMS LIKE " YOU'RE GOING TO POKE SOMEBODY'S EYE OUT WITH THAT."

WHY ARE YOU FOLLOWING ME AROUND?

WHY ARE YOU FOLLOWING ME AROUND?

AND WHY ARE YOU REPEATING WHAT I SAY?

AND WHY ARE YOU REPEATING WHAT I SAY?

IF YOU'RE GOING TO KEEP DOING THAT, I JUST WON'T SAY ANYTHING.

IF YOU'RE GOING TO KEEP DOING THAT, I JUST WON'T SAY ANYTHING.

THE INCREDIBLY ANNOYING HUMAN ECHO STRIKES AGAIN!

 I'M GOING TO PASTE SUSIE'S PATE WITH A SLUSHBALL! HEH HEH HEH!

   SOME PHILOSOPHERS SAY THAT *TRUE* HAPPINESS COMES FROM A LIFE OF VIRTUE.

 SOMEDAY I'LL WRITE MY *OWN* PHILOSOPHY BOOK. VIRTUE NEEDS SOME CHEAPER THRILLS.

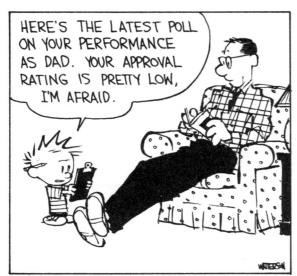

Test:

1. What important event took place on December 16, 1773?

I do NOT BELIEVE IN LINEAR TIME. THERE IS NO PAST AND FUTURE: ALL IS ONE, AND EXISTENCE IN THE TEMPORAL SENSE IS ILLUSORY. THIS QUESTION, THEREFORE, IS MEANINGLESS AND IMPOSSIBLE TO ANSWER.

WHEN IN DOUBT, DENY ALL TERMS AND DEFINITIONS.

YAAAAA

RRRR RR R

OK, IT'S HARDER THAN IT LOOKS.

GOODNESS, HOW DID YOU GUYS EVER LIVE LONG ENOUGH TO INVENT TOOLS?

DING DONG ♪

HEH HEH HEH!

OH! OOP!...UM...HI, MRS. DERKINS. I WAS HOPING SUSIE WOULD ANSWER THE...UH...I MEAN, UM, I'M SELLING HUGE SNOWBALLS. WOULD YOU LIKE TO BUY ONE?

MY "PLAN A's" ARE GREAT, BUT MY "PLAN B's" LEAVE A LOT TO BE DESIRED.

POW!

LOOK OUT!

MY SNOWBALLS GO FASTER THAN THE SPEED OF SOUND.

THEY DO NOT, YOU BIG LIAR!

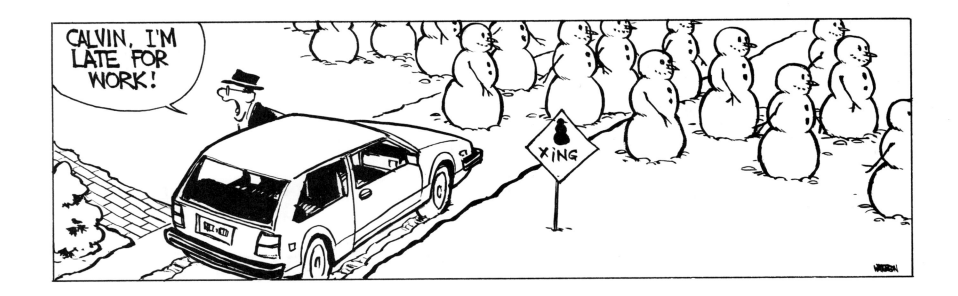

YES, CALVIN? WHY AREN'T YOU TEACHING US THE GENDERS OF NOUNS?

IS "DESK" MASCULINE? IS "CHAIR" FEMININE? FOREIGN KIDS KNOW, BUT *WE* DON'T! NO WONDER WE CAN'T COMPETE IN A GLOBAL MARKET! I DEMAND SEX EDUCATION!

..I WONDER IF HER DOCTOR KNOWS SHE MIXES ALL THOSE MEDICATIONS.

YAWWNN

TRIFLE NOT WITH TIRED TIGERS.

SHOULD I STAY INSIDE OR GO OUTSIDE?

IT'S AWFULLY COLD OUT, BUT I SUPPOSE I COULD BUNDLE UP. IT LOOKS WINDY THOUGH. BUT STILL, I'D LIKE TO GO SLEDDING. THEN AGAIN, MAYBE I'D RATHER STAY IN. ON THE OTHER HAND...

GO OUT AND CLOSE THE DOOR!

THE MORE INDECISIVE I AM, THE FASTER THINGS GET DECIDED.

I LIKE FOLLOWING THE NEWS! NEWS ORGANIZATIONS KNOW I WON'T SIT STILL FOR ANY SERIOUS DISCUSSION OF COMPLEX AND BORING ISSUES.

THEY GIVE ME WHAT I WANT: ANTICS, EMOTIONAL CONFRONTATION, SOUND BITES, SCANDAL, SOB STORIES AND POPULARITY POLLS ALL PACKAGED AS A SOAP OPERA AND HORSE RACE! IT'S VERY ENTERTAINING.

THEN COMMENTATORS WONDER WHY THE PUBLIC IS CYNICAL ABOUT POLITICS.

YOU CAN TELL THIS IS AN IN-DEPTH STORY, BECAUSE IT'S GOT AN ARTICLE NEXT TO THE CHART.

I SAW A SIGN ON A RESTAURANT DOOR THAT SAID, "NO SHIRT, NO SHOES, NO SERVICE."

BUT IT DIDN'T SAY ANYTHING ABOUT *PANTS!* IF I WENT IN WEARING SHOES AND A SHIRT, BUT NO PANTS, THEY'D HAVE TO SERVE ME!

THEY'D PROBABLY SERVE YOU WITH A COURT SUMMONS.

C'MON, LET'S SEE IF MOM WILL TAKE US OUT FOR DINNER!

THERE!

WHATCHA DOIN'?

I'VE HIDDEN A CACHE OF SNOWBALLS BEHIND EVERY TREE IN THE YARD!

NOW WHEN MY ENEMIES COME AFTER ME, I NEED ONLY RUN TO THE NEAREST TREE TO BE INSTANTLY ARMED.

INGENIOUS.

NOW I NEED TO MAKE SOME ENEMIES.

I'LL BE ONE.

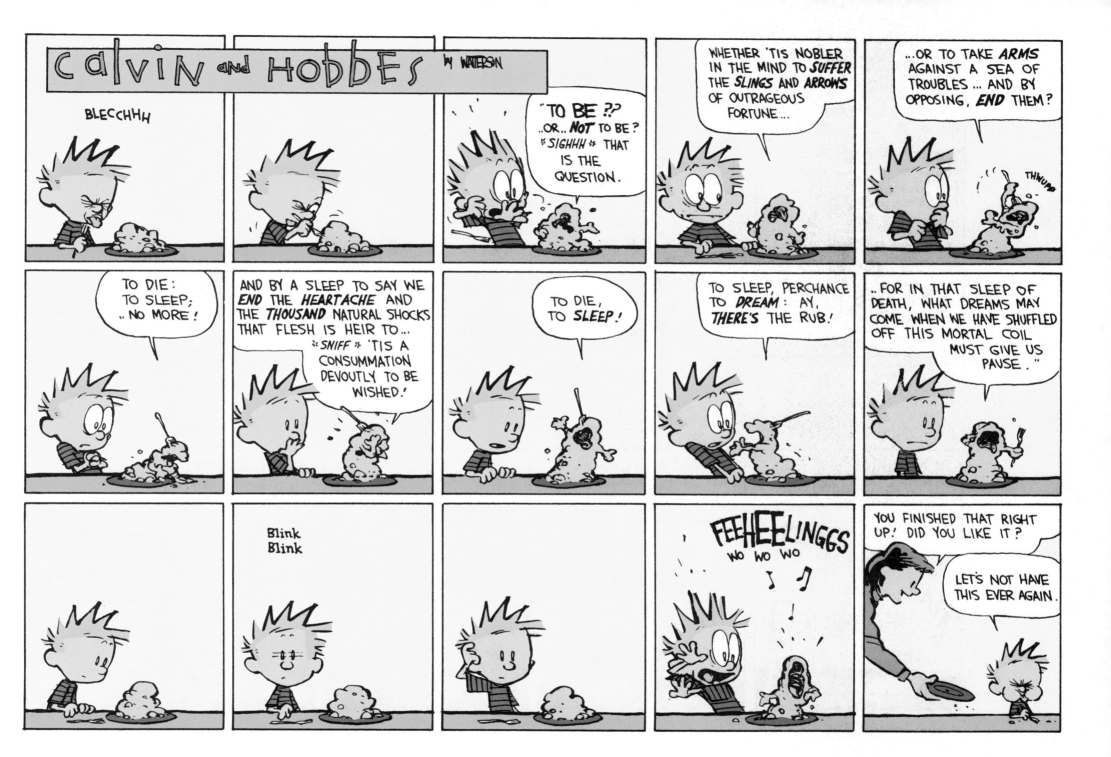

TIME TO GET UP, CALVIN.

IS IT A SNOW DAY? DID THEY CLOSE THE SCHOOLS?

I'VE GOT THE RADIO ON, SO WE'LL HEAR. GET READY ANYWAY, THOUGH.

OH MAN, I HOPE I HOPE I HOPE!

IF SCHOOL'S CLOSED, I'LL HAVE THE WHOLE DAY TO DO THE MATH HOMEWORK I FORGOT YESTERDAY. IF SCHOOL'S OPEN, I'M IN BIG TROUBLE.

SUDDENLY I FEEL EXTREMELY RELIGIOUS.

ANOTHER DEATHBED CONVERSION.

HA HA! THEY JUST ANNOUNCED THE SCHOOLS ARE CLOSED! IT'S A SNOW DAY! **WHEEEEEEE!**

YES! YES! YES! YES!

TALK ABOUT LUCK! NOW YOU CAN DO YOUR HOMEWORK AND YOU WON'T GET IN TROUBLE!

RIGHT, BUT THERE'S OVER TWO FEET OF SNOW THAT REQUIRES OUR IMMEDIATE AND UNDIVIDED ATTENTION.

FIRST THINGS FIRST.

MATH WILL STILL BE THERE WHEN THE SNOW MELTS.

DON'T YOU THINK YOU'D ENJOY THIS MORE IF YOU DID YOUR MATH ASSIGNMENT FIRST, SO IT WASN'T HANGING OVER YOUR HEAD?

I'M A PRACTICAL MAN, HOBBES. I DON'T WASTE TIME THINKING ABOUT HYPOTHETICAL SITUATIONS. I DEAL WITH THE WORLD HERE AND NOW.

AND THE INCONTROVERTIBLE FACT IS THAT I'M OUTSIDE IN THE SNOW! *THAT'S* REALITY! *THAT'S* WHAT I THINK ABOUT!

TOMORROW'S A REALITY TOO.

HYPOTHETICALLY, IT MIGHT BE ANOTHER SNOW DAY.

WHAT A BUSY DAY! I'M POOPED!

MOM SAYS THE ROADS ARE PRETTY CLEAR, SO SCHOOL WILL PROBABLY OPEN AGAIN TOMORROW.

NOW I WISH I'D DONE MY MATH HOMEWORK INSTEAD OF PLAYING OUTSIDE ALL DAY.

...OR I WISH I'D DONE IT BEFORE DINNER ... OR AFTER DINNER... OR INSTEAD OF WATCHING TV ... OR BEFORE BED. BUT NOW IT'S TOO LATE.

A DAY CAN REALLY SLIP BY WHEN YOU'RE DELIBERATELY AVOIDING WHAT YOU'RE SUPPOSED TO DO.

120

I'M DETERMINED TO SET THE WORLD RECORD FOR HAVING ONE'S FINGER CONTINUOUSLY IN ONE'S NOSE.

I CAN'T BELIEVE THERE'S EVEN SUCH A CATEGORY.

IN THAT CASE, CALL ME "CHAMP"!

THIS PIECE OF PIE IS AWFULLY DARN SMALL!

LIFE COULD BE WORSE, CALVIN.

LIFE COULD BE A LOT BETTER, TOO!

... BUT WORSE IS MORE LIKELY.

I'VE DECIDED I SUFFER FROM LOW SELF-ESTEEM.

IS THAT A FACT.

FROM NOW ON, MY GOAL IS TO FEEL GOOD ABOUT MYSELF.

YOU'RE GOING TO WORK HARDER AT EVERYTHING AND BUILD SOME CHARACTER?

NO, I'M GOING TO WHINE UNTIL I GET THE SPECIAL TREATMENT I LIKE.

I WONDER IF ANYONE ELSE IS AS SCARED ABOUT THE FUTURE AS I AM.

I'VE FOUND THAT IMMEDIATE GRATIFICATION IS THE ONLY THING THAT HELPS ME.

EWWW! WHAT'S THIS, SOMETHING SCRAPED OFF THE BOTTOM OF BOOTS?? I'M NOT EATING IT!

CALVIN, I MADE THIS LAST WEEK AND YOU SAID IT WAS YOUR FAVORITE MEAL OF ALL TIME AND YOU WISHED WE COULD HAVE IT EVERY DAY FOR THE REST OF YOUR LIFE!

WELL, NOW I HATE IT.

ANOTHER DAY, ANOTHER GRAY HAIR FOR MOM!

I'M HO-OOAAUGH!!

KAPOW!

MAN, WAS THIS CAT A-PULTED! HEE HEE HEE!

YOU'RE A RIOT, HOBBES.

THESE COLORS REALLY AREN'T ENOUGH, SO I HAVE TO MIX SOME TO GET THE SPECIFIC HUES I NEED.

SEE, HERE I START WITH A LAYER OF BROWN. THEN I ADD OLIVE GREEN AND SCRUB A LITTLE ORANGE AND YELLOW OCHRE INTO IT. FINALLY, I TOP IT WITH LIME GREEN, PURPLE, AND TAN.

WOW, PERFECT BARF!

YOU'D THINK THAT WOULD BE A STANDARD COLOR IN A BIG SET LIKE THIS.

WHEN IT SNOWS, YOU CAN GO SLEDDING. WHEN IT'S WINDY, YOU CAN FLY KITES. WHEN IT'S HOT, YOU CAN GO SWIMMING.

BUT WHEN IT'S RAINING... SIGH...

..THE ONLY SPORT IS DRIVING MOM CRAZY.

I THOUGHT I HAD A GREAT IDEA, BUT IT NEVER REALLY TOOK OFF.

IN FACT, IT DIDN'T EVEN GET ON THE RUNWAY.

I GUESS YOU COULD SAY IT EXPLODED IN THE HANGAR.

I'VE HAD IDEAS LIKE THAT.

HOW ARE YOU DOING ON YOUR NEW YEAR'S RESOLUTIONS?

I DIDN'T MAKE ANY.

SEE, IN ORDER TO IMPROVE ONESELF, ONE MUST HAVE SOME IDEA OF WHAT'S "GOOD." THAT IMPLIES CERTAIN VALUES.

BUT AS WE ALL KNOW, VALUES ARE RELATIVE. EVERY SYSTEM OF BELIEF IS EQUALLY VALID AND WE NEED TO TOLERATE DIVERSITY. VIRTUE ISN'T "BETTER" THAN VICE. IT'S JUST DIFFERENT.

I DON'T KNOW IF I CAN TOLERATE THAT MUCH TOLERANCE.

I REFUSE TO BE VICTIMIZED BY NOTIONS OF VIRTUOUS BEHAVIOR.

NO! NO! NO! I NEED MORE SLEEP!

I C-CAN'T KEEP M-MY EYES OPEN!

BED?! ALREADY?? BUT I'M WIDE AWAKE!!

MY INTERNAL CLOCK IS ON TOKYO TIME.

I SURE AM GREAT! I'M ONE OF THE GREATEST PEOPLE WHO EVER LIVED!

HOW LUCKY PEOPLE ARE TO KNOW SOMEONE AS GREAT AS ME! I'M GREAT IN SO MANY GREAT WAYS! IN FACT, I'M SO GREAT THAT MY GREATNESS IS...

YOU'RE NOT GREAT! YOU'RE THE MOST CONCEITED BLOWHARD I'VE EVER MET!

WHEN YOU'RE GREAT, PEOPLE OFTEN MISTAKE CANDOR FOR BRAGGING.

HERE, I'LL HANG UP YOUR COAT.

THANKS.

IF YOU'VE BEEN LOOKING FOR HOBBES, HE SOMEHOW GOT PUT IN THE CLOSET. I JUST FOUND HIM WAY BACK IN THERE.

WAITING FOR ME IN THE *CLOSET*, EH? TOO BAD YOUR LITTLE PLAN WAS *THWARTED!!*

WHY DON'T YOU HANG UP YOUR COAT YOURSELF?!

Calvin and Hobbes by Watterson

NEXT, ON EYEWITNESS ACTION NEWS: BLOOD-SPATTERED SIDEWALKS AND SHROUD-COVERED BODIES! COULD THE NEXT VICTIM BE *YOU*??

WE'LL GET THE STORY FROM THE LIVING ROOMS OF SOBBING, HYSTERICAL RELATIVES AND WE'LL TELL YOU WHY *YOU* SHOULD BE PARALYZED WITH HELPLESS FEAR!

THAT'S EYEWITNESS ACTION NEWS! IT'S WHAT *YOU* NEED TO *KNOW*!

WHEN I GROW UP, I'M GOING TO BE A SCIENTIST.

I'LL DEDICATE MY CAREER TO THE PROPOSITION THAT MAN CAN RESHAPE THE UNIVERSE ACCORDING TO HIS OWN WHIMS.

I'LL PROBABLY GO INTO GENETIC ENGINEERING AND CREATE NEW LIFE FORMS.

YOU WANT TO PLAY GOD?

NOT EXACTLY. GOD NEVER BOTHERED TO PATENT HIS STUFF.

SOME DAYS YOU GET UP AND YOU ALREADY KNOW THAT THINGS AREN'T GOING TO GO WELL.

THEY'RE THE TYPE OF DAYS WHEN YOU SHOULD JUST GIVE IN, PUT YOUR PAJAMAS BACK ON, MAKE SOME HOT CHOCOLATE, AND READ COMIC BOOKS IN BED WITH THE COVERS UP UNTIL THE WORLD LOOKS MORE ENCOURAGING.

OF COURSE, THEY NEVER LET YOU DO THAT.

IS TODAY ONE OF THOSE DAYS?

IT SURE IS!!

ON GRAY DAYS, WHEN IT'S SNOWING OR RAINING, I THINK YOU SHOULD BE ABLE TO CALL UP A JUDGE AND TAKE AN OATH THAT YOU'LL JUST READ A GOOD BOOK ALL DAY, AND HE'D ALLOW YOU TO STAY HOME.

SO YOU'D ONLY GO TO SCHOOL ON SUNNY DAYS?

WELL NO, ON SUNNY DAYS THE JUDGE WOULD LET YOU PLAY OUTSIDE.

HE'S QUITE A GUY.

HE'D MAKE YOU GO TO SCHOOL IF IT WAS HOT, HAZY, AND HUMID WITH A LOT OF BUGS.

139

Outta my way, Twinky.

.. AND SUDDENLY, THE EARTH OPENED UP! WAILING HELPLESSLY, MOE TUMBLED HEAD OVER HEELS DOWN THE SMOKING CHASM UNTIL HE SPLASHED INTO THE MOLTEN MAGMA AT THE PLANET'S CORE, WHERE HE SLOWLY MELTED BEFORE IGNITING IN A SPITTING FIREBALL OF GREASE!

HOW IN THE WORLD DID YOU GET IN TO THE BATHROOM AND BACK OUT SO FAST?

THIS SCULPTURE WILL BE CALLED "THE SPIRIT OF COMPROMISE." WE'LL EACH MAKE A SNOWMAN AND HAVE THEM SHAKING HANDS.

GREAT.

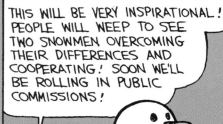

THIS WILL BE VERY INSPIRATIONAL! PEOPLE WILL WEEP TO SEE TWO SNOWMEN OVERCOMING THEIR DIFFERENCES AND COOPERATING! SOON WE'LL BE ROLLING IN PUBLIC COMMISSIONS!

calvin and HobbES
by WATTERSON

MAKE YOUR SNOWMAN'S ARM LONGER. HIS HAND WON'T REACH MY SNOWMAN'S HAND.

WHY SHOULD I MAKE A NEW ARM? JUST MAKE YOURS LONGER.

THEN IT WILL LOOK LIKE MY SNOWMAN HAD TO REACH FARTHER THAN YOURS DID. THEY SHOULD BE EQUAL.

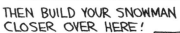

THEN BUILD YOUR SNOWMAN CLOSER OVER HERE!

I'M NOT GOING TO START ALL OVER! JUST MAKE YOUR ARM LONGER!

I REFUSE! YOU CAN'T TELL ME WHAT TO DO!

IN THAT CASE, MY SNOWMAN REFUSES TO SHAKE WITH YOUR SNOWMAN!

SO WHAT!! MY SNOWMAN WON'T EVEN TALK TO YOURS! I'M TURNING HIS HEAD THE OTHER WAY!

HA! WHILE HE'S LOOKING OVER THERE, MY SNOWMAN WILL KICK YOUR SNOWMAN IN HIS BIG WHITE BUTT!

OH YEAH?! WELL MINE KNOCKS YOUR SNOWMAN'S HEAD OFF!

FINE! MY SNOWMAN FEEDS YOUR SNOWMAN HIS OWN NOSE!

WHY YOU..!!

OW

LEGGO

OOF

STOP IT!

I DON'T THINK THIS SCULPTURE IS VERY GOOD.

IT'S A COMPROMISE.

144

CalViN and HobbEs *by WATTERSON*

ONE OF MY BABY TEETH CAME OUT!

I HAVE TO SAY, I'M NOT ENTIRELY COMFORTABLE HOLDING A PIECE OF MY OWN HEAD.

MOM SAYS THE TOOTH FAIRY MIGHT GIVE ME 50 CENTS FOR THIS TOOTH.

WOW!

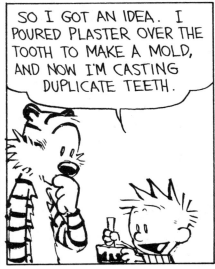

SO I GOT AN IDEA. I POURED PLASTER OVER THE TOOTH TO MAKE A MOLD, AND NOW I'M CASTING DUPLICATE TEETH.

I'LL PUT ONE UNDER THE PILLOW EVERY NIGHT, AND BY THE END OF THE YEAR, I'LL HAVE OVER 150 DOLLARS!

DO YOU THINK THE TOOTH FAIRY WILL BELIEVE YOUR MOUTH HAD 300 TEETH IN IT?

IF SHE'D RATHER HAVE AN OLD TOOTH THAN 50 CENTS, HOW BRIGHT CAN SHE BE?

MMM... SOMEBODY'S HAVING A FIRE. I LOVE THE SMELL OF A FIRE ON A COLD WINTER DAY.

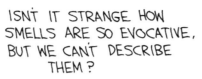

ISN'T IT STRANGE HOW SMELLS ARE SO EVOCATIVE, BUT WE CAN'T DESCRIBE THEM?

OH, I DUNNO. THAT FIRE HAS A SNORKY, BRAMBISH SMELL.

I SHOULD HAVE KNOWN ANIMALS WOULD HAVE WORDS FOR SMELLS.

IT'S A LITTLE BRUNKY, BUT THE LOW HUMIDITY AFFECTS THAT.

YOU'RE TELLING ME THAT ANIMALS HAVE THEIR OWN WORDS FOR SPECIFIC SMELLS?

WELL SURE.

OK, WHAT'S THE WORD FOR HOW WET LEAVES SMELL?

"SNIPPID."

WHAT'S THE WORD FOR HOW *I* SMELL?

"TERRIBLE."

WOO HOO HOO HOO HO

GRAPHIC VIOLENCE IN THE MEDIA.

DOES IT GLAMORIZE VIOLENCE? SURE. DOES IT DESENSITIZE US TO VIOLENCE? OF COURSE. DOES IT HELP US TOLERATE VIOLENCE? YOU BET. DOES IT STUNT OUR EMPATHY FOR OUR FELLOW BEINGS? HECK YES.

DOES IT *CAUSE* VIOLENCE? ...WELL, THAT'S HARD TO PROVE.

THE TRICK IS TO ASK THE RIGHT QUESTION.

MOST PEOPLE DON'T KNOW WHAT IT'S LIKE TO BE A CHILD PRODIGY, SO THAT'S WHY I'M WRITING MY AUTOBIOGRAPHY.

DOES YOUR MAGNANIMITY KNOW NO BOUNDS?

GENIUS HAS ITS OBLIGATIONS.

HEY, HOW DO YOU SPELL "BOOGERS"?

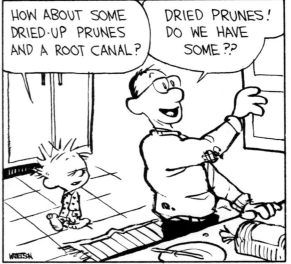

155

WITH SHEER BRAIN POWER, I WILL FORCE THIS SLED TO CARRY ME UP THE HILL!

BUT UNTIL I DECIDE TO DO THAT, I'LL WALK!

I WONDER WHY PEOPLE ARE NEVER CONTENT WITH WHAT THEY HAVE.

ARE YOU KIDDING? YOUR FINGERNAILS ARE A JOKE, YOU'VE GOT NO FANGS, YOU CAN'T SEE AT NIGHT, YOUR PINK HIDES ARE RIDICULOUS, YOUR REFLEXES ARE NIL, AND YOU DON'T EVEN HAVE TAILS! OF COURSE PEOPLE AREN'T CONTENT!

FORGET I SAID ANYTHING.

NOW IF *TIGERS* WEREN'T CONTENT, THAT WOULD BE SOMETHING TO WONDER ABOUT.

I LIKE HOMEWORK. HOMEWORK MAKES ME HAPPY.

I DON'T WANT TO GO OUTSIDE. I WANT TO DO MATH PROBLEMS.

BLEHHH

MY BRAIN ALWAYS REJECTS ATTITUDE TRANSPLANTS.

LOOK AT HOW PEOPLE ARE PORTRAYED IN COMIC STRIPS. THE WOMEN ARE INDECISIVE WHINERS, NAGGING SHREWS, AND BIMBOS!

AND THE MEN ARE NO BETTER. THEY'RE BEFUDDLED MORONS, HEAVY DRINKERS, GLUTTONS, AND LAZY GOOF-OFFS! EVERYONE IS INCOMPETENT, UNAPPRECIATED, AND UNSUCCESSFUL!

WHAT KIND OF INSIDIOUS SOCIAL PROGRAMMING IS THIS?! NO WONDER THE WORLD'S SUCH A MESS! I DEMAND POLITICALLY CORRECT, MORALLY UPLIFTING ROLE MODELS IN THE FUNNIES!

YES, WE ALL KNOW HOW FUNNY GOOD ROLE MODELS ARE.

AND LOOK, ALL THE KIDS ARE OBNOXIOUS BRATS!

WOULDN'T IT BE COOL IF YOU SNEEZED AND THE SPRAY FROM YOUR NOSE INSTANTLY FROZE?

YOU COULD BREAK IT OFF YOUR FACE AND HAVE A 3-D SCULPTURE OF YOUR SNEEZE!

...WELL, I THINK IT WOULD BE COOL.

PEOPLE WONDER WHY CATS ARE SOLITARY.

CALVIN, STOP RUNNING THROUGH THE HOUSE!

THE LAW IS ON THE BOOKS, BUT IT WOULD TAKE ALL THEIR RESOURCES TO ENFORCE IT.

CALVIN!

160

VROOOOMM
BEEP BEEP BEEP BEEP

SPLUTCHH

ACKK! NOT SO MUCH! NOT SO MUCH! I HATE THIS STUFF!

PIPE DOWN AND EAT.

What happened in Concord in 1775?

LET'S BE HONEST. YOU'RE ASKING ME ABOUT CONCORD? I RELY ON THE BUS DRIVER TO FIND MY OWN HOUSE FROM HERE. CONCORD COULD BE ON NEPTUNE FOR ALL I KNOW.

AND WHAT HAPPENED 220 YEARS AGO?? I'M A KID. I DON'T KNOW WHAT'S GOING ON NOW. I DON'T HAVE A SHRED OF CONTEXT FOR ANY OF THIS. IT'S HOPELESS, MISS WORMWOOD, HOPELESS.

WE BOTH TRY TO DEMORALIZE EACH OTHER.

LOOK HOBBES, THIS IS MY RETIREMENT FUND.

A COMIC BOOK?

THIS IS THE ISSUE WHERE THEY INTRODUCE THE ARCH-VILLAIN "DEATHMEISTER"! IN A FEW YEARS, A RARE MINT COPY OF THIS WILL BE WORTH MILLIONS OF DOLLARS!

NEEDLESS TO SAY, I BOUGHT FIVE COPIES, SEALED THEM IN AIRTIGHT PLASTIC BAGS, AND PUT THEM IN A BOX IN THE CLOSET, WHERE THE LIGHT AND HUMIDITY WON'T AFFECT THEIR PRECIOUS PAGES!

HOW WILL THESE BE RARE AND VALUABLE IF EVERY KID IN AMERICA HAS FIVE COPIES?

WE'RE ALL COUNTING ON THE OTHER GUY'S MOM TO THROW THEM AWAY.

IF I HAD A COMPUTER, I'M SURE I'D GET BETTER GRADES ON MY BOOK REPORTS.

YOU'D STILL HAVE TO READ THE BOOK AND TELL THE COMPUTER WHAT YOU WANT TO SAY, YOU KNOW.

MAN, WHAT'S ALL THE FUSS ABOUT COMPUTERS?!

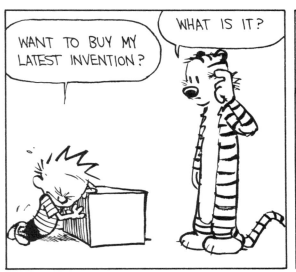

SOMETIMES ALL THAT FELINE DIGNITY IS JUST TOO MUCH TO KEEP UP.

TODAY FOR "SHOW AND TELL," I REFUSE TO SHOW YOU WHAT I BROUGHT AND I REFUSE TO TELL YOU ANYTHING ABOUT IT!

IT'S A MYSTERY THAT WILL HAUNT YOU ALL YOUR MISERABLE LIVES! YOU'LL NEVER, *EVER* KNOW WHAT I BROUGHT! YOU CAN BEG AND PLEAD, BUT I'LL NEVER END YOUR TORMENT!

I'LL CARRY MY SECRET TO THE GRAVE! IT'S THE SHOW AND TELL THAT WAS NEVER SHOWN OR TOLD! HA HA HA! AH HA HA HA HA!

EVERYBODY WANTS THE SAME OLD THING.

OK, THAT'S PLENTY OF TELEVISION. TURN IT OFF.

I'LL MOPE AND WHINE AND ARGUE! I'LL GET IN THE WAY! I'LL GET IN TROUBLE! I'LL TEAR AROUND! YOU WON'T HAVE A MOMENT'S PEACE IF YOU MAKE ME TURN OFF THE TV!

I NOTICED SHE HAD TO THINK ABOUT IT.

HELLO? YES, I'D LIKE TO SPEAK WITH THE CHIEF OF POLICE.

HELLO, CHIEF? IS IT A **LAW** THAT YOUR SOCKS HAVE TO MATCH ANYTHING ELSE YOU'RE WEARING?

HEY MOM, LISTEN TO THIS!

I LIKE TO SET KITES FREE.

SOMETIMES WHEN I'M TALKING, MY WORDS CAN'T KEEP UP WITH MY THOUGHTS.

I WONDER WHY WE THINK FASTER THAN WE CAN SPEAK.

PROBABLY SO WE CAN THINK TWICE.

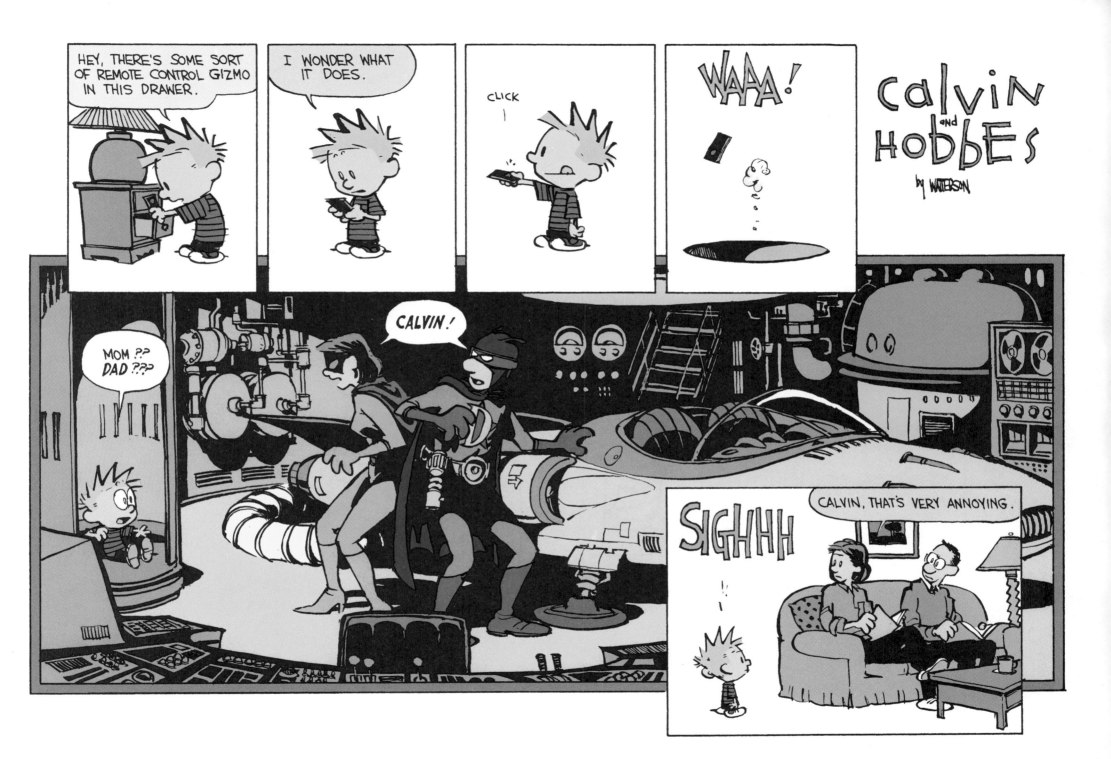

175